W9-CCQ-449

★ SPORTS STARS ★

DEREK JETER
SHORTSTOP SENSATION

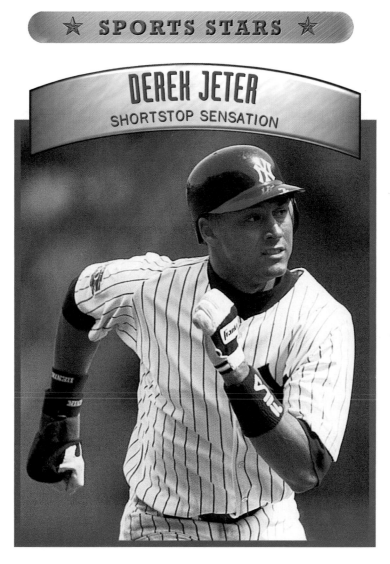

BY BRENDAN JANUARY

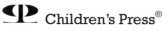 Children's Press®
A Division of Grolier Publishing
New York London Hong Kong Sydney
Danbury, Connecticut

Photo Credits

Photographs ©: Allsport USA: 37 (Vincent Laforet), 36 (Doug Pensinger); AP/Wide World Photos: 42 (Lynsey Addario), 25 (Richard Drew), 39 (Ron Frehm), 26, 43, 45 left (Mark Lennihan), 32 (Suzanne Plunkett), 12 (Nick Wass); Barbara Jean Germano: 23 (Baseball Weekly); Corbis-Bettmann: 41, 45 right (Reuters Newmedia Inc.); Icon Sports Media: 3, 29, 46 (David Seelig); Jim McLean: 19; John Klein: cover, 30; SportsChrome East/West: 6, 44 right, 47 (Rob Tringali Jr.); Tony Dugal: 11, 16, 44 left; Tyler Bolden: 20, 35.

Visit Children's Press® on the Internet at:
http://publishing.grolier.com

Library of Congress Cataloging-in-Publication Data

January, Brendan, 1972–
    Derek Jeter / by Brendan January.
        p. cm. — (Sports stars)
        Summary: Discusses the personal life and baseball career of the young man from Michigan who achieved his dream to play shortstop for the New York Yankees.
        ISBN 0-516-22046-2 (lib. bdg.)   0-516-27071-0 (pbk.)
        1. Jeter, Derek, 1974---Juvenile literature. 2. Baseball players—United States—Biography—Juvenile literature. [1. Jeter, Derek, 1974- 2. Baseball players. 3. Racially mixed people—Biography.] I. Title. II. Series.

GV865.J48 J25   2000
                                    00-020672

© 2000 by Children's Press®, a Division of Grolier Publishing Co., Inc.
All rights reserved. Published simultaneously in Canada.
Printed in the United States of America.
    4 5 6 7 8 9 10 R 09 08 07 06 05 04 03

CONTENTS

★ 1 ★

YANKEE SUPERSTAR

In the lights of Yankee Stadium, Derek Jeter digs his spikes into the soft dirt of the batter's box. On the mound, the pitcher leans into his windup and hurls a fastball over the outside corner of the plate. Derek swings, extending his arms powerfully. He makes contact—but the ball slices foul. The pitcher throws another pitch—a belt-high fastball over the inside of the plate. Derek swings again. This time he pulls his hands in and makes contact. The ball sails in a high arc over the grasping second baseman and falls safely into right field. On the next pitch, Derek breaks for second base, causing the second

baseman to cover the bag. The hitter slaps
the ball into the open hole, and Derek rounds
second and goes to third. The next hitter hits
a deep fly ball. Derek tags at third and scores
on the sacrifice.

The crowd roars with excitement as Derek's
teammates tap fists with him in congratulation.
The opposing pitcher shakes his head. Derek
fought off one of his best pitches, helped execute
a hit and run, and scored on a sacrifice fly. There
seems little that a pitcher, or any of the other
teams in the league, can do to stop Derek Jeter.

★ 2 ★

RAISED A YANKEE

Derek wasn't born a Yankee, but he was raised to be one. Born on June 26, 1974, Derek spent his early childhood in West Milford, New Jersey, a town near New York City. Derek's mother, Dorothy, was one of fourteen children, so Derek grew up surrounded by family—most of them die-hard Yankees fans. Family gatherings often turned into rooting sessions for their beloved team, especially while the Yankees were winning the World Series in 1977 and 1978.

When Derek was five years old, the Jeter family moved to Kalamazoo, Michigan, but Derek remained loyal to the Yankees. In his new room, Derek tacked up a poster of his idol—

Yankees' outfielder David Winfield. During summer vacation, Derek visited his relatives in New Jersey and spent most of his nights in New York at Yankee Stadium.

In Kalamazoo, Derek not only watched baseball, but he also learned to play it. Next to the Jeter house lay the high school athletic fields. Charles Jeter—Derek's father—along with Derek, his mother, and his sister, Sharlee, would grab their bats, balls, and gloves and run out to the baseball diamond. Dorothy pitched Wiffle balls to Derek. Charles hit ground balls to Derek and Sharlee.

Watching his son field and throw, Charles realized that Derek had talent. When he was young, Charles had played shortstop at Fisk University in Tennessee and dreamed of becoming a professional ballplayer. He loved the game, but loving it and having fun weren't enough. It took discipline and hard work to succeed.

Charles was determined to teach this lesson to Derek and Sharlee. Every year, Charles, Dorothy,

Derek has had a passion for baseball since he was young.

Derek has always striven to achieve exceptional goals.

and their children prepared a contract. The parents listed the goals they expected Derek and Sharlee to achieve in the coming year—in grades, athletics, and other projects. Derek wanted to play baseball, but his schoolwork came first. "Derek had goals," Dorothy said, "but he knew if he wanted to play in the Little League all-star game or go to baseball camp, he better come home with a 4.0, he better have his behavior intact, and he better make curfew—or he wasn't going anywhere."

Charles constantly challenged his son, forcing him to strive and achieve. When Derek began playing Little League baseball, he hoped to play shortstop as his father had. But Charles, the coach of the team, ordered Derek to play second base. Derek's face filled with disappointment. Charles would let his son play shortstop, but only after he earned it.

Charles taught his son not to blame others for setbacks. When Derek struck out on a called third strike, he complained loudly and looked to

———————— ★ ★ ★ ————————

his father for help. Charles showed no sympathy: What about the first two pitches you swung at and missed?

Whenever Derek and Charles played a game, his father always tried to win. "If it was checkers, it didn't matter," remembered Derek. "I just wanted to beat him. That's why I'm so competitive. He had no mercy on me. He never let up on me."

Derek's competitive attitude inspired him to make lofty goals. At a game in Detroit, he announced to his family that he would play there someday as a major leaguer. His parents listened seriously and assured Derek that he was right—if he was willing to work for it.

"A lot of people's parents would have told them to be more realistic," Derek said. "But my parents always felt if I worked hard enough I could make any dream come true." Derek's parents weren't the only ones who believed in him. In eighth grade, Derek's classmates voted him "Most likely to play shortstop for the New York Yankees."

HIGH SCHOOL STAR

Derek made the varsity baseball squad at Kalamazoo Central High School after his first season. Over the next three years, he grew stronger and more skilled. His throwing arm became so powerful that Derek's coach was forced to replace the first baseman. "Derek would throw the ball 91–92 miles an hour from short to first," explained the coach. "I had to put a better athlete at first just to handle his throws."

Derek honed his skills in the off-season. During the winter, he played basketball to stay in shape. In the summer, he played baseball with a local team, the Maroons.

★ ★ ★

Even though Derek devoted hours to sports, he remained a serious student. By the end of his last year in high school, Derek faced a difficult decision. He had maintained an exceptional 3.82 grade average. Derek and his parents decided that an education was too important to put off. After he graduated, Derek planned to attend a university and study medicine.

But Derek's play on the baseball diamond had attracted national attention. More than 30 major-league scouts crowded the stands every game to watch him play. In his senior year, Derek hit .508. In 23 games, he smacked 30 hits, including 5 doubles, 4 home runs, and a triple.

Derek was voted the 1992 High School Player

Derek was a popular ball-player even when he was in high school. During his senior year, major-league scouts constantly went to watch him play.

16

of the Year by the American Baseball Coaches Association. With this honor, it was no longer a question of whether he would be drafted into the major leagues, but which team would draft him.

It seemed likely that Derek would be selected by the Houston Astros or the Cincinnati Reds, but neither team excited Derek. The Reds already had an established shortstop, and Derek didn't want to play backup. As draft day approached, Derek accepted a baseball scholarship from the University of Michigan.

Then, on the day of the draft, the phone rang. "My mom answered and said that the Yankees were on the phone," he said. "I can't even describe how I felt." Cincinnati and Houston had decided to select other players, leaving the Yankees to pick Jeter. After a discussion with his parents, Derek agreed to sign with the Yankees, but only if they agreed to pay for his education at the University of Michigan. The Yankees immediately agreed. Two weeks after high school graduation, Derek packed his bags to join the Yankees rookie league team in Tampa, Florida.

★ 4 ★

MINOR-LEAGUE
SENSATION

Alone for the first time in his life, 18-year-old
Derek was miserable. He telephoned his
family every night. Although he spent only eight
weeks in that league, Derek felt as if it were
eight months. He hit a meager .202.

"I struggled in rookie ball," Derek said. "I
didn't know anybody. There was no one to turn
to. Everything was new to me. My family was
so far away."

Derek's coaches weren't concerned with
his low batting average, because most young
ballplayers struggle to adjust to minor-league
pitching. But they were alarmed at Derek's poor
play at shortstop. Eager to impress the coaches,

Derek on the Greensboro Hornets in 1993

Derek was rushing to ground balls and throwing wildly. In 1993, he averaged nearly one error every two games. Derek had special difficulty catching up with balls hit up the middle. His confidence shattered, Derek called home. "You have to go from game to game," advised

Derek during the brief period he played for the Yankees in the minor leagues

his father. "You can't let your game fall apart because of one bad play."

Derek went to the Yankees special instructional league, where he learned how to position his feet and hands before throwing to first. The next season, Derek concentrated on improving his skills from one game to the next. He grew more comfortable at the plate, raising his average to .295.

Then, in 1994, Derek broke out. He batted .329 in class A. The Yankees promoted him to AA, where Derek pounded opposing pitchers and increased his average to .377. After spending enough time to earn Player of the Month, Derek jumped to AAA—only one step away from the major league. Derek hit .349, with 9 triples and 45 RBIs in just 35 games.

At the end of the season, Derek was voted Minor League Player of the Year by *Baseball America*, *The Sporting News*, and *USA Today Baseball Weekly*. No one could remember when a player had conquered the Yankees minor league system in just two months.

Derek eagerly awaited the call that would send him to the Yankees. But the 1994 season ended in August, when the players and the owners were quarreling over contracts, and the players refused to play. For the first time since 1904, the World Series was canceled.

Derek had to wait until the 1995 season to get his chance. When the Yankees' shortstop, Tony Fernandez, pulled a muscle in his rib cage in May, the Yankees called up Derek.

Derek, just 20, was the youngest player in the American League (A.L.). In his first three games, Derek hit 3 for 11 and made no errors. The Yankees' manager, Buck Showalter, was impressed by Derek's baseball skill and his personality. "The first thing that jumps out at you," he said, "is very obviously the quality job his dad and mom have done with him. It's very refreshing to see the things they have taught him in life carry over to the big leagues."

To Derek's great disappointment, the Yankees returned him to the minor leagues in June. They didn't want to hurry their young star before he was ready. In September, Derek was called up again. Again, Derek impressed the Yankees' coaches and his fellow players with his defensive skills and his improved hitting.

In 1996 spring training, Fernandez suffered a season-ending injury. After three years in the minor leagues, Derek became the Yankees' starting shortstop.

Derek was very disappointed when he was sent back down to the minors in the 1995 season, but his big chance was soon to come.

★ 5 ★

ROOKIE OF THE YEAR

The new Yankees' manager, Joe Torre, did not have high expectations for his young shortstop in the 1996 season. "The only thing that I require and hopefully come to expect is that he play solid defense," said Torre.

From the start, Derek provided offense and defense. On opening day at Yankee Stadium, he smashed a pitch over the left-field fence for his first major-league home run. In the field, Derek was dazzling, snaring a hopping ground ball to his right and later making an over-the-shoulder basket catch. "That was a major-league play," said Yankees' pitcher David Cone after the game.

Derek with the Yankees' manager, Joe Torre (left), and the team's owner, George Steinbrenner (right)

In the first game of the 1996 American League Championship Series, a fan interfered with the Orioles' attempt to catch Derek Jeter's fly ball, which was ruled a home run.

"I think right then and there, we all learned something about Derek."

Derek also became comfortable at the plate. By mid-July, he was batting .284. Then he began a streak, hitting in 17 straight games—just missing the 18-consecutive-game streak for a rookie set by Yankee legend Joe DiMaggio. In mid-August, Derek was hitting .314.

The Yankees eventually won the eastern division and defeated Texas in the divisional playoffs. But to advance to the World Series, the Yankees had to go through their division rivals— the Baltimore Orioles.

In the first game, the Orioles gained a 4–3 lead. In the eighth inning, Derek hit a high fly ball to right field. The Orioles' right fielder scrambled to the wall to make the catch. Suddenly, a 12-year-old fan named Jeffrey Maier rushed up to the fence and put out his glove. The ball skipped out of his grasp and into the seats. The umpire signaled a home run. As the Orioles' manager and players protested furiously, Derek rounded the bases. The Yankees won the game in extra innings and went on to win the series. After the series, the Orioles complained that Derek's hit and Maier's interference had changed the entire course of the playoffs.

Derek paid no attention to the criticism. He had hit .412 in the series and played a major role in several rallies, a performance that awed Coach Torre. "He has an uncommon sense of things," said Torre. "Very polished. Sometimes he surprises me with the things he says and does. It's hard to believe he's twenty-what? One? Two? Three?"

In the World Series, the Yankees faced the defending champion—the Atlanta Braves. After losing the first two games in Yankee Stadium, the Yankees went to Atlanta and won three games. They returned to New York and defeated the stunned Braves to win their first World Series since 1978. The city went wild with celebrations.

Derek immediately earned the respect of his teammates by his incredible performances in the field.

Derek's pleasant personality and good looks have produced many new female fans.

"This year has just been a fantasy, a dream come true," said Derek. "You just couldn't have written a better script if you'd been in Hollywood." At the victory parade held among the skyscrapers of Manhattan, Derek drew most of the cheers. Among the sea of people, many young women waved signs urging Derek to marry them. Teammates teased Derek by imitating the shrill, excited screams of his adoring fans.

"I find it hard to believe," said Derek about the attention. "I'm just an average guy who plays baseball for a living." No one else thought of Derek as average, though. He finished the season batting .314, including 10 home runs, 78 RBIs, and 104 runs. Even more important to Derek, he made only 22 errors in 178 games. The Baseball Writers Association of America voted him American League Rookie of the Year.

It had been an incredible year of achievement, but Derek was most proud of what he did after the season. In December, he announced the establishment of the Turn 2 Foundation. Turn 2 would donate money to steer young people away from the destruction of drugs and alcohol. Derek's father, an experienced drug counselor with a Ph.D. in sociology, is executive director of the foundation. Derek is chief operating officer.

"People look up to you if you play for the Yankees," said Derek. "I think you should do something to help out. Some players don't look at it that way. Off the field is when people look up to you even more. That's when your job starts. Baseball is the easy part."

Derek has become one of the most popular Yankees. Here, he signs autographs outside Yankee Stadium.

Because of his great rookie year, Derek had become the most popular Yankee. Four out of every five Yankee fan letters were addressed to him, and they came so quickly that they piled up in his locker. Other fans created websites in his honor. Derek didn't take the attention too seriously but instead focused on becoming a better ballplayer for the 1997 season.

"It's easy for me to improve on last year," he said. "I made a lot of mistakes. I need to run more, steal more bases, make less errors, and be a smarter hitter. I struck out too much last year, more than 100 times."

Derek started the 1997 season well but then fell into a terrible slump. The season frustrated Derek and the Yankees. The Orioles seized the lead in the division, and the Yankees had to settle for the wild-card berth. After leading the Cleveland Indians two games to one in the divisional playoffs, the Yankees lost two games in a row, ending their season.

After that bitter loss, Derek bought a house in Tampa, near the Yankees' training complex. He would have no off-season. During the winter, he lifted weights and altered his swing so that he could turn on inside fastballs. Working every day on a batting tee, he learned to stand straight, allowing him the flexibility to whip his bat at inside pitches. Pitchers who threw inside would get a nasty surprise next season.

✦ 6 ✦

THE BEST EVER

The Yankees started the 1998 season angered by their 1997 failure and determined to prove that 1996 was not a fluke. After losing four of their first five games in the season, the team began beating opposing teams at an astonishing rate. By mid-May, they were 28–9, the second-best start ever by a Yankee team.

Derek was a big contributor to their success. His .316 average, 94 hits, and 10 home runs landed him on the All-Star team. By the end of the season, the Yankees had won 114 games and cruised into the post-season. Derek continued his All-Star form, finishing the year with a .324 average—30 points higher than the

Derek (right) and his teammates Scott Brosius (left) and Paul O'Neill (center) played for the American League at the 1998 All-Star game.

last season. He finished third in balloting for the league Most Valuable Player (MVP), behind Texas Rangers right-fielder Juan Gonzalez and Boston Red Sox shortstop Nomar Garciaparra.

During the post-season, the Yankees swept the Rangers in the divisional playoffs and then faced the Cleveland Indians in the American League Championship Series (A.L.C.S.). In Game Six, the Yankees were clinging to a 6–5 lead in the sixth

Derek is congratulated by his teammates after he scores a run against the San Diego Padres in the fourth and final game of the 1998 World Series.

inning when Derek stepped up to the plate. The pitcher threw a hanging curveball that Derek lined into the right-field corner for a triple. Derek then scored on a single by Bernie Williams. After the game, the Indians' shortstop, Omar Vizquel, commented that Derek's triple ended the series. "It was a knife to the heart," he said.

The Yankees faced the surprising San Diego Padres in the World Series. Derek, who struggled with a .176 average through the first two rounds of the playoffs, hit .353 in the series. The Yankees won the first three games. In the fourth game, Derek went two for four and scored two of the Yankees' three runs. The Yankees swept the four-game series to win their 24th World Series and finish their season with an unbelievable 125–50

record. "I'm a little too young to know about the teams from the early 1900s," said Derek, "but we were 125 and 50, and there's not too many teams that can say that."

The Yankees celebrate their 24th World Series win in 1998 after sweeping the four-game series.

★ 7 ★

YOUNG VETERAN

It would have been easy for Derek to relax after 1998. He had already won two World Series rings, more than most players have after a long career. But Derek had no intention of letting up. He began the 1999 season by hitting close to .400. His average fell lower, but he finished the season with an astounding .349 average, second only to Boston Red Sox shortstop Nomar Garciaparra, who won the batting title with a .357 average.

More important, Derek had become a true team leader. Even older players were inspired by his carefree but disciplined approach to the game.

"I think Derek is going to become the best player I've ever been on the same team with,"

Jason Wood is forced out at second base as Derek Jeter jumps over him during a game against the Detroit Tigers in 1999.

said Yankees' right-fielder Paul O'Neill. "It's amazing how much he's improved and how many things he can do as a hitter now . . . he's incredible."

The Yankees dominated their division and entered the playoffs for the fifth year in a row. In the divisional playoffs, the Yankees swiftly stepped over the Texas Rangers in a three-game sweep and then beat the Boston Red Sox four games to one.

In the World Series, the Yankees faced the Atlanta Braves—their opponent in 1996. In Game One, Derek collected two hits off Atlanta ace Greg Maddux. The second hit, with bases loaded, tied the score and knocked Maddux out of the game. Paul O'Neill then hit a single off reliever John Rocker that put the Yankees ahead for good. The Braves didn't recover from the shocking defeat, and the Yankees won the next three games to seize their 25th World Championship.

After five years in major-league baseball, Derek had won his third World Series ring and was recognized as one of the game's best players. In New York City, he had become a celebrity, attracting attention and causing a stir wherever

Derek sprays fans with champagne after the Yankees defeat the Atlanta Braves in another four-game sweep of the World Series in 1999.

Derek cheers atop a float with some teammates during the 1999 ticker-tape victory parade in New York City.

he appeared. The New York *Daily News* listed the best Yankees to ever play at each position. It picked Joe DiMaggio in center field, Babe Ruth in right field, and Derek Jeter at shortstop. One columnist renamed Yankee Stadium from "The House That Ruth Built" to "The House That Derek Will Rebuild."

"He's very, very special for his age," said Yankees' owner George Steinbrenner. "His upbringing shows on him every day. He brings tribute to himself, the Yankees, and his family."

Derek proudly stands under a sign quoting Yankee legend Joe DiMaggio after the Yankees win their 25th World Series.

C ★ H ★ R ★ O ★ N

1974 • June 26: Derek is born in Pequannock, New Jersey.

1992 • Derek hits .508 as a senior in Kalamazoo, Michigan, and is named High School Player of the Year. The Yankees select Jeter in the first round of the draft.

1994 • Derek advances rapidly through the Yankees' minor-league system. *Baseball America*, *The Sporting News*, and *USA Today Baseball Weekly* vote Derek the Minor League Player of the Year.

1995 • The Yankees call up Derek to play 13 games but send him back down in June. Derek returns in September and hits .250.

O ★ L ★ O ★ G ★ Y

1996 • Derek hits a home run in his first opening-day game. He finishes the season hitting .314 and wins the A.L. Rookie of the Year Award.

1997 • The Yankees win the wild-card spot in the playoffs but lose to the Cleveland Indians.

1998 • Derek bats .324 and finishes third in votes for the league's MVP. His 19 home runs set a record for single-season home runs held by a Yankee shortstop. The Yankees sweep the San Diego Padres to win the World Series.

1999 • Derek bats .349, second behind Nomar Garciaparra at .357 for the league batting title. The Yankees sweep the Atlanta Braves for their 25th World Series Championship.

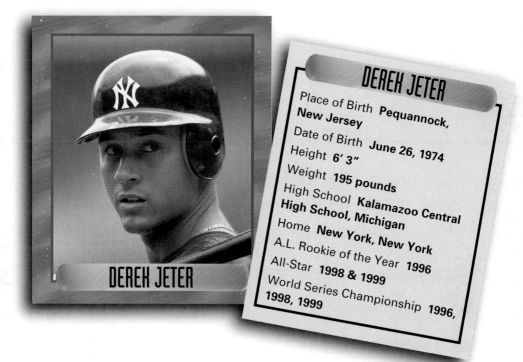

DEREK JETER

Place of Birth **Pequannock, New Jersey**

Date of Birth **June 26, 1974**

Height **6′ 3″**

Weight **195 pounds**

High School **Kalamazoo Central High School, Michigan**

Home **New York, New York**

A.L. Rookie of the Year **1996**

All-Star **1998 & 1999**

World Series Championship **1996, 1998, 1999**

★ MAJOR LEAGUE STATISTICS ★

Year	Team	Runs	Hits	Home Runs	RBI	Batting Average
1995	New York Yankees	5	12	0	7	.250
1996	New York Yankees	104	183	10	78	.314
1997	New York Yankees	116	190	10	70	.291
1998	New York Yankees	127	203	19	84	.324
1999	New York Yankees	134	219	24	102	.349
Totals	(5 seasons)	486	807	63	341	.318

ABOUT THE AUTHOR

Brendan January was born and raised in Pleasantville, New York. He is a graduate of Haverford College and the Columbia Graduate School of Journalism. A sports and American history enthusiast, he has written several books for Children's Press. Mr. January is currently a journalist at *The Philadelphia Inquirer*.